Did You

LINC

A MISCELLANY

Compiled by Julia Skinner

With particular reference to the work of Craig Spence

THE FRANCIS FRITH COLLECTION

www.francisfrith.com

Based on a book first published in the United Kingdom in 2004 by The Francis Frith Collection®

Hardback edition published in 2008 ISBN 978-1-84589-391-0
Text and Design copyright The Francis Frith Collection®
Photographs copyright The Francis Frith Collection® except where indicated.

British Library Cataloguing in Publication Data

Did You Know? Lincoln - A Miscellany
Compiled by Julia Skinner
With particular reference to the work of Craig Spence

The Francis Frith Collection
Frith's Barn, Teffont,
Salisbury, Wiltshire SP3 5QP
Tel: +44 (0) 1722 716 376
Email: info@francisfrith.co.uk
www.francisfrith.com

Printed and bound in Singapore

Front Cover: **LINCOLN, STEEP HILL 1923** 74640p

The colour-tinting is for illustrative purposes only, and is not intended to be historically accurate

CONTENTS

4   Introduction

6   Lincolnshire Words, Phrases & Folklore

8   Haunted Lincoln

13   Lincoln Miscellany

42   Sporting Lincoln

44   Quiz Questions

48   Recipes

50   Quiz Answers

54   Francis Frith - Pioneer Victorian Photographer

LINCOLN, STONEBOW 1901 46773

3

INTRODUCTION

What is now Lincoln was established as a Roman legionary fortress by AD68. The legionary fortress occupied the area of the present castle and minster and immediately north. This was laid out subsequently as the basis of the Roman walled town, which became a 'colonia', or settlement for retired Roman legionaries. It thus acquired the name 'Lindum Colonia', and subsequently in Anglo-Saxon times this name changed from 'Lindocolonia' to 'Lyndcylene' and then to Lincoln.

In the Anglo-Saxon period Lincoln was in the Anglian kingdom of Lindsey which was absorbed by the kingdom of Mercia in the 7th century, and then became part of the Danelaw, the area of England under Danish (or Viking) control, becoming one of the 'Five Boroughs'. English re-conquest under King Edward the Elder ended Danish rule by AD920, and by the time of the Domesday Book in 1086 Lincoln was a wealthy trading town and one of the most important in England.

After the Norman Conquest the area of the Roman walled town became the site of the castle, and the rest of this area became its outer bailey or forecourt. A third of the area within the walls was cleared of houses for the great castle to be raised, and much Norman stonework survives in the core of the present walls. Lincoln's most significant building, the cathedral, also had its origins in the eleventh century, but a rebuild was necessitated by a spectacular earthquake in 1185; from this tragedy one of Europe's most impressive and beautiful medieval cathedrals emerged, initially under St Hugh of Avalon, bishop from 1186 to 1200.

There are many superb historic buildings within the cathedral close and throughout the upper town, not least the Stonebow medieval gateway and guildhall, and High Bridge carrying its timber-framed houses. The most remarkable survivals of the earlier medieval city are the Norman House, the Jew's House and, to the south, St Mary's Guildhall - these are rare 12th-century medieval secular stone buildings. Besides these, there are of course numerous later medieval buildings, many with timber-framing either exposed or concealed within later Georgian and Victorian brick casings.

However, Lincoln's great glory is the cathedral, which dominates the uphill area of the city and was aptly described by the poet Robert Southey: 'Never was an edifice more happily placed, overtopping a city built on the activity of a steep hill'.

LINCOLN, BRAYFORD POOL 1890 25620

LINCOLNSHIRE WORDS, PHRASES & FOLKLORE

'Yellowbelly' - a term for someone born and bred in Lincoln. There are many theories about the origin of the name, but one of the favourite explanations is that it derives from the bright yellow waistcoat which was worn by the 10th Regiment of Foot, later The Lincolnshire Regiment.

'Gimmer' - a ewe (female sheep) which has never given birth.

'Frim folk' - people from another area.

'Reasty' - rancid.

'Chunter' - to complain.

'Starnil' - a starling.

'Kecks' - trousers.

'Mardy' - bad tempered, sulky.

'Kelch' - mud.

'Wick' - lively.

'Wassack' or **'Gump'** - a fool.

'Jiffle' - fidget.

'Yucker' - a young person.

'Throng' - busy.

'Uneppen' - clumsy.

'Proggle' - to poke about (with a stick)

On 'Mumping Day'- or St Thomas's Day, 21st December - it was the custom in Lincolnshire for poor people to go around begging for Christmas fare.

It was an old Lincolnshire belief that when a baby was born with noticeably large ears, it was a sign that he or she would be successful in life.

LINCOLN, ST MARY'S CHURCH AND CONDUIT 1890 25661

HAUNTED LINCOLN

One of Lincoln's many ghosts is that of 'Clarke's Hound', a lurcher dog originally owned by a poacher called William Clarke who was sentenced to death for murdering a gamekeeper. Whilst Clarke was awaiting execution in Lincoln Castle his dog was looked after at The Strugglers Inn, and after he was hanged the dog pined away and died. The dog's body was stuffed and is now on show in Lincoln Castle, but its ghost is said to roam the area around the castle walls looking for its master and is sometimes heard scratching and barking at the pub door as well.

A phantom rolling head is reported to bounce down the steep area of Greestone Steps, and knocks down anyone not quick enough to move out of the way!

The Green Dragon public house is said to be haunted by the pipe-smoking ghost of Mary Cooper, who worked in the building before it became a pub. Mary has been blamed for all manner of strange events, such as broken bottles being found and beer pumps being unaccountably turned off.

A ghostly young boy known as Humphrey is said to haunt Brown's Pie Shop, running around and causing mischief. The ghost of a young girl is also said to roam the building.

The White Hart Hotel is said to be one of the most haunted buildings in Lincoln. One of its most gruesome ghosts is that of a porter at the hotel who was also a highwayman. He suffered a horrible injury when a hold-up went wrong and a coachman thrust a flaming torch into his face, burning part of it away. He hid himself away whilst his injuries healed, but eventually he went mad with the pain and shot himself. His ghost now haunts the former stables of the hotel, now the Orangery restaurant, hiding his damaged face behind his cloak. Another ghost at the hotel is known as 'the Mobcap Girl'. She was a maid at the hotel who caught the eye of the local ratcatcher, but he murdered her in a fit of anger when she rebuffed his attentions. The unfortunate girl's ghost is now said to haunt the first-floor landing.

LINCOLN, STONEBOW 1923 74634

LINCOLN MISCELLANY

The River Witham was the site of religious rituals dating back into the Bronze Age. It may still have been a focus for spiritual activity when the Romans arrived in the area in the AD50s.

The Roman legionary fortress built by the Ninth Legion Hispana just before AD68 was a vast complex incorporating a headquarters building, officers' houses, barracks and stables among other structures. It probably housed somewhere in the region of 5,000 men.

The name Lincoln derives from the shortening and joining of the two names given to the city about AD86. At that time the city was designated as a Colonia, a special settlement for legionary veterans. Its earlier name, of Celtic-British origin, was Lindum meaning a settlement by a pool or lake. So 'Lindum Colonia' eventually became Lincoln.

The Roman city's main administrative building was the basilica located in the centre of the upper city. This was a massive masonry structure that covered an area of around 900 square metres. It has been estimated that the building stood well over nine metres high. An important fragment of the basilica survives in the form of the 'Mint Wall'.

One branch of Lincoln's Roman aqueduct arrived at the north wall of the city a little to the east of the Newport Arch. Here it emptied into a great masonry water tank that held around 12,000 litres of water. This probably helped to supply the demands of the public baths complex situated just to the south.

The most important road junction in Lincoln was actually some 700 metres south of the city. Here the Fosse Way joined with Ermine Street amid a cluster of timber built shops and workshops. Part of the road surface of the Fosse Way can be seen today preserved under a glass floor within the medieval St Mary's Guildhall.

In the third century Lincoln became the capital city of the new Roman province of Britannia Secunda. During the 19th century a huge and elaborately decorated villa of third century date was discovered, and destroyed, some distance to the east of the city near Greetwell Lane. Was this the residence of the new provincial governor?

Later Roman Lincoln has provided strong evidence for the presence of a Christian community. In 1972 the remains of an early church were excavated on the site of St Paul in the Bail. The importance of this religious community was demonstrated by the church's symbolic placing within the centre of the Roman forum.

LINCOLN, STEEP HILL 1923 74640

LINCOLN, AERIAL VIEW FROM SOUTH WEST c1960 L49088

LINCOLN, THE STRAIT c1960 L49122

By the later Saxon period Lincoln must have been a city of rubble, ruin and decay. The older Roman street grid had been so lost that new thoroughfares, such as Silver Street, were created that ignored it completely.

Under Danish rule Lincoln became a wealthy place. During the 10th and 11th centuries the city was home to some 95 moneyers who all produced coin; only London could boast a greater number.

The earliest Norman 'castle' in Lincoln comprised the whole of the upper city, re-using the Roman walls and gates. The castle as we now recognise it having been constructed at the beginning of the 12th century.

Countess Lucy de Taillebois was Sheriff of Lincoln until her death in 1136; she was a remarkable woman who was granted the office in her own right having outlived three husbands. The Lucy Tower in Lincoln Castle is named after her.

After the cathedral was partially destroyed by an earthquake in 1185, a plea was made for funds to help rebuild it. A poor man from Stow offered all his meagre savings to the project. Hearing of his generosity Bishop Hugh noted that he would be rewarded in heaven where all were equal. To represent this a statue of Bishop Hugh was placed on the pinnacle of the right-hand corner tower of the west front, while on the left-hand tower the Swineherd of Stow stands at exactly the same height.

Only four 'copies' of the Magna Carta dating from 1215 still survive, one of which belongs to Lincoln Cathedral. It is on display in a special exhibition inside Lincoln Castle.

High Bridge was enlarged following the murder of Thomas Becket, Archbishop of Canterbury, to allow a chapel dedicated to St Thomas to built on its eastern side. The chapel stood until the 18th century.

LINCOLN CATHEDRAL, THE FONT c1965 L49138

During the 1820s widening works on the River Witham revealed French swords and armour, no doubt belonging to soldiers who discarded them or drowned in a desperate attempt to cross to safety during the 'Battle of Lincoln Fair' in 1217.

At the southern limits of the medieval suburb of Wigford stood Great Bargate and Little Bargate, but which was the largest? Little Bargate of course!

Lincoln's City Council is still called to its meetings in a chamber above the Stonebow by the ringing of the 'mote bell', which was cast in 1371. The Stonebow was the southern gateway of the medieval city.

The fortified walls and gates of the Cathedral Close were constructed over a period of years during the 13th and 14th centuries. The Close remained legally independent of the city until 1835.

Henry VIII must have been very impressed with the sumptuous decoration of the cathedral during his visit of 1541 as in 1542 he sent his officials to confiscate its wealth. They came away with a huge quantity of precious jewels, 122 kilos of silver and 74 kilos of gold.

Between 1311 and 1548 the spire that surmounted Lincoln Cathedral's central tower made it the highest building in the world.

LINCOLN, JEW'S HOUSE 1890 25664

The local interpretation of the Statute of Artificers of 1563 required all those in need of work to present themselves outside the Stonebow each morning and to stand for an hour in the hope of being hired, failure to comply would result in imprisonment.

In the aftermath of the English Civil War battle for Lincoln in 1643 the plundering of the city became so frenzied that the Commons were obliged to take action. They had to issue a formal order forbidding the removal of lead or bells from churches and houses throughout the city.

The north side of the cathedral cloister was severely damaged during the English Civil War. In 1674 it was rebuilt to house the cathedral library in a classical design created by Sir Christopher Wren.

During the 18th century Lincoln had two Assembly Halls. The first was built on Bailgate in 1745 to entertain the social elite of the upper city. The second was built in 1757 and was constructed above the Butter Market on the High Street by the commercial elite of the lower city.

LINCOLN, GREEN DRAGON HOTEL c1960 L49130

A regular feature of the Lincoln social calendar was the Stuff Ball. Started in 1789 to provide support for the local woollen cloth trade, those attending wore clothes made of Lincolnshire 'stuff'. The patron

MUMBY & SON Ltd.
NEWARK.
LEEDS.
LINCOLN.
WHOLESALE
CLOTHIERS

GIRLS WANTED

of the event was Lady Banks, wife of Sir Joseph Banks, native of Lincolnshire and the naturalist who accompanied Captain Cook on his first voyage to the South Seas.

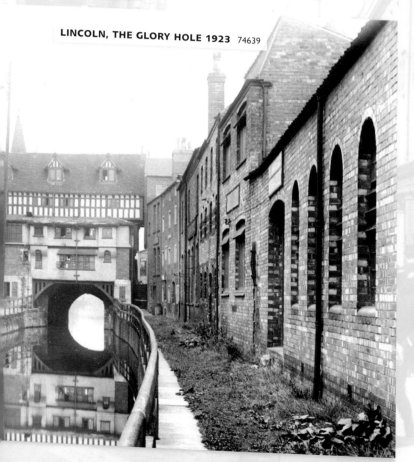

LINCOLN, THE GLORY HOLE 1923 74639

LINCOLN, THE CATHEDRAL FROM BRAYFORD c1965 L49230

In 1801 Lincoln's population was about 7,000; a century later it had grown to just under 49,000.

George Boole, the author of the theory of Boolean Logic and pioneer of binary notation, and hence one of the pioneers of the modern computer age, was born in Silver Street in 1815, the son of a shoemaker. He spent his twenties working as a schoolmaster and lecturer in the city.

In 1822 the Governor of Lincoln Gaol, John Merriweather, added the small circular turret to the top of the Observatory Tower. The addition was built to house the governor's astronomical telescope hence the name, however others suggested it was built for him to 'observe' the women prisoners in the exercise yard below.

In 1836 a massive Wesleyan Chapel was constructed on Claskegate. It was able to seat 1,400 and became known as 'Big Wesley'. It was demolished in 1963.

In the 19th century Colonel Charles Sibthorpe, Lincoln's eccentric Member of Parliament, in response to a wager drove a carriage and horses, known as a 'four-in-hand', down Steep Hill. After this dramatic if rather foolhardy incident a rail was placed at the top of the hill to stop others attempting the same.

The first steam train arrived in Lincoln in 1846 and soon after a level crossing was erected across the High Street. Today the level crossing survives, making Lincoln the largest city in England to have the traffic along its main town centre street interrupted several times an hour by passing trains.

Before the arrival of the railways an important steam packet paddle-boat service regularly journeyed from the centre of Lincoln along the River Witham to the port of Boston. The railways eventually put the service out of business.

The engineering firm of Clayton and Shuttleworth had such success at the Great Exhibition in 1851 they soon after became the largest manufacturer of steam engines and threshing machines in Britain.

For many years Lincoln's High Street was the venue for its famous Horse Fair. The event only moved from the city centre to West Common in 1929.

In 1872 huge crowds gathered to celebrate the opening of the Arboretum gardens on Monks Road. There were brass bands, bell ringers and dancing but no drinking, as the aim of the park was to tempt 'a man to enjoy himself with his wife and family in preference to the pleasure of the public house'.

LINCOLN, TENNYSON STATUE 1906 55109

LINCOLN, SCHOOL OF ART 1890 25663

One of the oldest businesses in Lincoln is the stationer and printer J Ruddock Ltd. Ruddock's moved into their present premises in the High Street in 1904 but the company was founded in 1884 through the purchase of an earlier printing business established in the 1760s.

In 1904 polluted drinking water in the city caused a typhoid epidemic that struck down more than a thousand people and killed 127.

1905 saw the last horse-drawn tram in Lincoln; instead the line was electrified using magnetic studs set into the road. This was an unreliable system and was replaced by overhead wires in 1919.

In 1911 armed militia went on patrol in Lincoln following a major riot, associated with the national railway strike, that had raged up and down the High Street.

LINCOLN, HIGH STREET c1950 L49016

Lincoln is well known as the 'birth-place' of the tank but its engineering works also made military aircraft during the First World War. Indeed at the height of the war Lincoln was one of the largest aircraft production sites in the world.

Following the First World War Ruston and Hornsby attempted to convert their aircraft works to motorcar production. They built very good cars that were also very expensive but the motor trade market was changing and perhaps inevitably in 1925 they ran out of orders and ceased production.

In 1924 part of Clayton and Shuttleworth's business was sold to Babcock and Wilcox who made mooring masts for the government's imperial airship service. Not long after, the famous R101 airship would be seen in the skies above Lincoln.

The church of St Peter-at-Arches that stood close to the Stonebow was demolished in the 1930s, but its Georgian walls and windows were re-used to construct the new church of St Giles within the housing estate of that name to the north of the city.

LINCOLN, THE CATHEDRAL, THE WEST DOOR c1879 12448

LINCOLN, THE CATHEDRAL, TAPESTRY IN BISHOP LINGLAND'S CHANTRY c1965 L49152

The towers of the cathedral were considered in danger of collapse in 1921 and an emergency programme of restoration work was undertaken over the following eleven years. The works cost the then enormous sum of £130,000.

The Lincoln firm of Ruston & Hornsby merged with the American firm of Bucyrus-Erie in 1930, thus forming the famous excavator manufacturing company of Ruston-Bucyrus. Just before the Second World War, Winston Churchill encouraged Ruston-Bucyrus to experiment with a gigantic trench-digging machine nicknamed 'Nellie'. Despite Churchill's enthusiasm, by the time war broke out the concept had become redundant.

Lincoln's connections with the Royal Air Force were confirmed when RAF Waddington, in 1959, and RAF Scampton, in 1993, were each granted the Freedom of the City of Lincoln.

The City of Lincoln is twinned with three other cities: Nuestadt an der Weinstrasse in Germany (1969), Tangshan in China (1988) and Port Lincoln in Australia (1991).

LINCOLN, THE ARBORETUM c1879 12496

SPORTING LINCOLN

Annual horse racing events in Lincoln began in 1680 and continued on Lincoln Heath until 1773, after which they were relocated to the West Commons. In time the races became a regular three-day meeting held each spring. The most celebrated race was the Lincolnshire Handicap, first run in 1849. The Lincoln races sadly came to an end in 1964, due to falling attendance and the ending of financial support from the Racing Levy Board. However the 'Lincoln Handicap', as it is now known, still takes place each spring, although it has been transferred to Doncaster racecourse where it remains central to the flat-racing calendar, being the opening race of the season.

Lincoln City FC moved to its current home at Sincil Bank in 1895 from its previous home at John O'Gaunt's Ground, just off the High Street.

Lincoln City FC have never made it further than the last sixteen in the FA Cup, but they have done so on three different occasions: 1886 (against Glasgow Rangers), 1888 (against Preston North End) and 1902 (against Derby County).

During the 1970s the fortunes of Lincoln City FC prospered under the management of a former player named Graham Taylor; moving on, he eventually rose to become the England Manager.

Lincoln City FC are nicknamed 'the Imps', but do you know the name of their female counterparts, Lincoln City LFC? The answer is - 'The Lady Imps'.

Paul Palmer, the British swimmer who won the silver medal in the 400 metres Freestyle event at the 1996 Olympics in Atlanta, USA, was born in Lincoln in 1974. He attended Lincoln Christ's Hospital School, and trained at the City of Lincoln Pentaqua Swimming Club.

LINCOLN, CATTLE MARKET AND CATHEDRAL c1950 L49043

QUIZ QUESTIONS

Answers on page 50.

1. Which famous royal mistress and ancestress of the present royal family is buried in Lincoln Cathedral?

2. What makes Lincoln's Newport Arch so special? (Seen in 25660 on page 51.)

3. What does the row of circles marked by stone setts in the surface of Bailgate represent?

4. Where in Lincoln would you find a Roman gravestone that was re-used by a Saxon named Eirtig to commemorate the founding of a church?

5. Lincoln's medieval weavers mainly produced four kinds of cloth. One type of cloth was Lincoln Green, famously worn by Robin Hood, but what were the other three called?

6. Where will you find the Lincoln Imp (seen opposite)?

7. What is so special about Lincoln's High Bridge?

8. For many years a row of windmills stood on the cliff edge west of Burton Road, of which only one now survives. What is it called?

9. The Poet Laureate Alfred, Lord Tennyson was born in 1809 in the Lincolnshire village of Somersby. In 1905 a statue of the poet was unveiled on Minster Green to the north of the cathedral. It shows Tennyson accompanied by his favourite dog - what was her name? (Seen in photograph 55109 on page 31.)

10. It is a well-known fact that a Lincoln company constructed the world's first armoured fighting vehicle - the first tank was designed in 1915 by Lieutenant W G Wilson and William Tritton who was managing director of Wm Foster Ltd, at the New Wellington Works on New Boultham Road. But why were these vehicles called 'tanks'?

LINCOLN, THE LINCOLN IMP c1955 L49078

Did You Know?
LINCOLN
A MISCELLANY

RECIPE

LINCOLN GINGER BISCUITS

Ingredients:
350g/12ozs self-raising flour
225g/8ozs sugar
2 teaspoonfuls bicarbonate of soda
115g/4ozs butter or margarine
2 teaspoonfuls ground ginger
2 teaspoonfuls golden syrup
1 beaten egg

Place all the dry ingredients in a bowl.

Heat the butter or margarine and golden syrup gently in a pan until the fat has melted, then pour over the dry ingredients and mix to a fairly stiff consistency, whilst slowly adding in the beaten egg. Roll small pieces of the dough in your hand to make balls about the size of a walnut.

Place each ball of dough on a greased baking sheet, making sure they are well spaced apart. Bake for 15-20 minutes at 180°C/350°F/ Gas Mark 4 until golden brown.

RECIPE

LINCOLNSHIRE PLUM BREAD

Ingredients:

450g/1lb strong white bread flour
15g/ ½ oz easy-blend yeast
1 teaspoonful ground cinnamon
1 teaspoonful ground allspice
1 pinch of salt
2 eggs, lightly beaten

4 tablespoonfuls of sugar
110g/4oz melted butter
115ml/4fl oz warmed milk
50g/2oz currants
50g/2oz sultanas
225g/8oz prunes, cut into small pieces

Mix together all the ingredients except the dried fruit, using either a food processor or mixing and beating by hand, until you have formed an even, pliable dough. Turn out on to a floured surface, and knead until smooth and elastic. Place the dough in a greased bowl, cover and leave in a warm room for about 1 hour, until the dough has risen to double its size.

Knock back the risen dough and knead it again whilst gradually adding the dried fruit until it is evenly distributed through the dough. Divide the dough in two, shape into loaves and place into two small (450g/1lb) greased and lined loaf tins. Cover and leave again in a warm place to prove (rise) until the loaves have doubled in size.

Pre-heat the oven to 190° C/375° F/Gas Mark 5. Place the loaf tins on a pre-heated baking sheet and bake for 40-50 minutes. Take the loaves out of the tins and return them to the oven for a further 5-10 minutes - they will be properly cooked when they sound hollow when tapped on the base.

QUIZ ANSWERS

1. Catherine Swynford, who became mistress to John of Gaunt, one of the sons of Edward III, and was mother to four of his children. One of these children was John Beaufort from whom all of England's succeeding royal families can be traced. Catherine died in 1405 and is buried in Lincoln Cathedral. Her extraordinary life story inspired Anya Seton's famous historical novel 'Katherine' (although the name of her heroine was inaccurately spelt with a K!).

2. Newport Arch (or Roman north gate), which stands at the northern end of Bailgate, is the only Roman gateway in Britain still used by road traffic.

3. The circles mark the position of the colonnade that ran along the eastern side of the Roman forum (or marketplace), forming a covered way or portico.

4. The stone is set within the western wall of the tower of St Mary of Wigford and records the dedication of the church by Eirtig 'to the glory of Christ and St Mary'.

5. As well as Lincoln Green there was Lincoln Grey, Lincoln Blanket and the most expensive of all - Lincoln Scarlet.

6. The Lincoln Imp is a stone carving in the form of a small diabolical creature which can be found at Lincoln Cathedral. The builders of the shrine of St Hugh wanted pilgrims to have in mind the ever-present danger of evil, so they included a reminder of the devil high up between two arches on the north side of the Angel Choir. The creature has become world-famous as 'The Lincoln Imp' and has become a symbol of Lincoln, especially after it was popularised as a tourist item during the Victorian period. (See photograph L49078 on page 45.)

7. Lincoln's High Bridge is the only medieval bridge in England to still have buildings on it.

8. It is called Ellis Mill, and was restored in 1977.

9. The dog was a Siberian wolfhound named Karenina.

10. Because the workmen who built the hulls of the first vehicles were told that they were building tracked water containers or 'water tanks' for the army, in order for the production of these new fighting vehicles to be kept secret.

LINCOLN, THE NEWPORT ARCH 1890 25660

FRANCIS FRITH

PIONEER VICTORIAN PHOTOGRAPHER

Francis Frith, founder of the world-famous photographic archive, was a complex and multi-talented man. A devout Quaker and a highly successful Victorian businessman, he was philosophical by nature and pioneering in outlook. By 1855 he had already established a wholesale grocery business in Liverpool, and sold it for the astonishing sum of £200,000, which is the equivalent today of over £15,000,000. Now in his thirties, and captivated by the new science of photography, Frith set out on a series of pioneering journeys up the Nile and to the Near East.

INTRIGUE AND EXPLORATION

He was the first photographer to venture beyond the sixth cataract of the Nile. Africa was still the mysterious 'Dark Continent', and Stanley and Livingstone's historic meeting was a decade into the future. The conditions for picture taking confound belief. He laboured for hours in his wicker dark-room in the sweltering heat of the desert, while the volatile chemicals fizzed dangerously in their trays. Back in London he exhibited his photographs and was 'rapturously cheered' by members of the Royal Society. His reputation as a photographer was made overnight.

VENTURE OF A LIFE-TIME

By the 1870s the railways had threaded their way across the country, and Bank Holidays and half-day Saturdays had been made obligatory by Act of Parliament. All of a sudden the working man and his family were able to enjoy days out, take holidays, and see a little more of the world.

With typical business acumen, Francis Frith foresaw that these new tourists would enjoy having souvenirs to commemorate their days out. For the next thirty years he travelled the country by train and by pony and trap, producing fine photographs of seaside resorts and beauty spots that were keenly bought by millions of Victorians. These prints were painstakingly pasted into family albums and pored over during the dark nights of winter, rekindling precious memories of summer excursions. Frith's studio was soon supplying retail shops all over the country, and by 1890 F Frith & Co had become the greatest specialist photographic publishing company in the world, with over 2,000 sales outlets, and pioneered the picture postcard.

FRANCIS FRITH'S LEGACY

Francis Frith had died in 1898 at his villa in Cannes, his great project still growing. By 1970 the archive he created contained over a third of a million pictures showing 7,000 British towns and villages.

Frith's legacy to us today is of immense significance and value, for the magnificent archive of evocative photographs he created provides a unique record of change in the cities, towns and villages throughout Britain over a century and more. Frith and his fellow studio photographers revisited locations many times down the years to update their views, compiling for us an enthralling and colourful pageant of British life and character.

We are fortunate that Frith was dedicated to recording the minutiae of everyday life. For it is this sheer wealth of visual data, the painstaking chronicle of changes in dress, transport, street layouts, buildings, housing and landscape that captivates us so much today, offering us a powerful link with the past and with the lives of our ancestors.

Computers have now made it possible for Frith's many thousands of images to be accessed almost instantly. The archive offers every one of us an opportunity to examine the places where we and our families have lived and worked down the years. Its images, depicting our shared past, are now bringing pleasure and enlightenment to millions around the world a century and more after his death.

For further information visit: www.francisfrith.com

INTERIOR DECORATION

Frith's photographs can be seen framed and as giant wall murals in thousands of pubs, restaurants, hotels, banks, retail stores and other public buildings throughout Britain. These provide interesting and attractive décor, generating strong local interest and acting as a powerful reminder of gentler days in our increasingly busy and frenetic world.

FRITH PRODUCTS

All Frith photographs are available as prints and posters in a variety of different sizes and styles. In the UK we also offer a range of other gift and stationery products illustrated with Frith photographs, although many of these are not available for delivery outside the UK – see our web site for more information on the products available for delivery in your country.

THE INTERNET

Over 100,000 photographs of Britain can be viewed and purchased on the Frith web site. The web site also includes memories and reminiscences contributed by our customers, who have personal knowledge of localities and of the people and properties depicted in Frith photographs. If you wish to learn more about a specific town or village you may find these reminiscences fascinating to browse. Why not add your own comments if you think they would be of interest to others? See **www.francisfrith.com**

PLEASE HELP US BRING FRITH'S PHOTOGRAPHS TO LIFE

Our authors do their best to recount the history of the places they write about. They give insights into how particular towns and villages developed, they describe the architecture of streets and buildings, and they discuss the lives of famous people who lived there. But however knowledgeable our authors are, the story they tell is necessarily incomplete.

Frith's photographs are so much more than plain historical documents. They are living proofs of the flow of human life down the generations. They show real people at real moments in history; and each of those people is the son or daughter of someone, the brother or sister, aunt or uncle, grandfather or grandmother of someone else. All of them lived, worked and played in the streets depicted in Frith's photographs.

We would be grateful if you would give us your insights into the places shown in our photographs: the streets and buildings, the shops, businesses and industries. Post your memories of life in those streets on the Frith website: what it was like growing up there, who ran the local shop and what shopping was like years ago; if your workplace is shown tell us about your working day and what the building is used for now. Read other visitors' memories and reconnect with your shared local history and heritage. With your help more and more Frith photographs can be brought to life, and vital memories preserved for posterity, and for the benefit of historians in the future.

Wherever possible, we will try to include some of your comments in future editions of our books. Moreover, if you spot errors in dates, titles or other facts, please let us know, because our archive records are not always completely accurate—they rely on 140 years of human endeavour and hand-compiled records. You can email us using the contact form on the website.

Thank you!

For further information, trade, or author enquiries
please contact us at the address below:

**The Francis Frith Collection, Frith's Barn, Teffont,
Salisbury, Wiltshire, England SP3 5QP.**
Tel: +44 (0)1722 716 376 Fax: +44 (0)1722 716 881
e-mail: sales@francisfrith.co.uk **www.francisfrith.com**